Learning from Longhorns

Learning from Longhorns

Lester Galbreath *and* Glenn Dromgoole

Illustrations by Charles Shaw
Photographs by Watt M. Casey, Jr.

BRIGHT SKY PRESS
Box 416
Albany, Texas 76430

10 9 8 7 6 5 4 3 2 1

Library of Congress Cataloging-in-Publication Data

Galbreath, Lester, 1946–
        Learning from Longhorns / by Lester Galbreath and
        Glenn Dromgoole ; illustrations by Charles Shaw ;
        photographs by Watt M. Casey, Jr.
            p. cm.
        ISBN 1-931721-44-0 (alk. paper)
1. Texas longhorn cattle—Anecdotes. 2. Conduct of life—
Anecdotes. 3. Galbreath, Lester,
1946– I. Title: Longhorns. II. Dromgoole, Glenn. III. Title.

SF199.T48G35 2004
636.2'8—dc22
                                        2004054565

Book and cover design by Isabel Lasater Hernandez
Printed in China through Asia Pacific Offset

Contents

Photography Essay by Watt Matthews Casey, Jr.

Introduction

A LIVING LEGEND

NO TWO THINGS ARE AS SYMBOLIC of the American West—its heritage, its courage, its strength—as the Texas Longhorn and the American cowboy. They are partners on the Western stage, inextricably linked forever in history, folklore, and culture.

A true American, born and bred on the Texas ranges, the Texas Longhorn earned its place in the history of the state and nation. And today it continues to connect the past with the present. The Longhorn is truly a *living legend.*

I have been learning from Longhorns for more than thirty years as manager of the State of Texas Longhorn Herd, which now numbers more than a hundred-and-twenty-five head.

In this book, I want to share some things I have learned from my association with these very special animals. Many of the distinctive qualities and traits that apply to the Longhorn can also be applied to our own lives, whether those lives are lived on the rural or the urban ranges we roam.

I hope you will come away from these little life lessons with a keener appreciation for how the Texas Longhorn has impacted our history and continues to influence us even today.

This book owes its genesis to the vision and encouragement of Rue Judd, publisher of Bright Sky Press and a fervent fan of the Texas Longhorn. Glenn Dromgoole, who has written incisively about dog, cat, and horse behavior, helped formulate and shape the views expressed here. Charles Shaw's graceful sketches and watercolors and Watt Casey's photographs illuminate the passages and pay tribute to the majesty of the Longhorn.

Learning from Longhorns

BE PROUD OF YOUR HERITAGE

ONE OF THE FIRST LESSONS we can learn from the Longhorn is to be proud of our heritage. Wherever we come from, there is something rich and colorful in our past if we will take the time and trouble to study it, research it, and embrace it.

The Texas Longhorn serves as a vivid example. Its ancestors can be traced back to Christopher Columbus, who introduced Spanish cattle into the New World on his second voyage to Santo Domingo in 1493. The cattle made their way into Mexico and across the Rio Grande into what is now Texas in the late 1600s and early 1700s. Over the years, the Spanish cattle developed through survival of the fittest, absorbing the few herds of other breeds brought in by the first Texas settlers. What evolved was a wild, tough, sturdy, long-horned breed that would become known after the Civil War as the Texas Longhorn.

By the end of the Civil War, millions of Longhorn cattle roamed wild, providing a marketable commodity for a devastated Texas economy. Over the next twenty years, more than ten-million head of Texas Longhorns were rounded up and driven hundreds of miles north over the Goodnight-Loving Trail, the Chisholm Trail, and the Western or Dodge City Trail to markets in Kansas. They were trekked to Colorado, Wyoming, Montana, the Dakotas, and Canada.

The cattle drives energized the Texas economy, gave birth to the ranching industry, which has had such a huge influence on the state's history and culture, and introduced forever into the international spotlight that other legendary Western icon, the American cowboy.

We will touch on other aspects of Longhorn heritage throughout the book. The point here is that if we scratch deep enough into our own family histories, we too can find stories that illuminate and enrich and give meaning to our lives. Be proud of your heritage.

2

Read a Good Book

That might sound like a strange life lesson to draw from observing cattle. But I want to make a point right up front—and pay tribute to an excellent book that has had a huge influence on my life and to the great man who wrote it.

The best book ever written about the Texas Longhorn is *The Longhorn,* by the legendary Western author, J. Frank Dobie. I read the book when I began managing the State Herd in 1972, and from time to time I go back and read it again. When it was written in 1941, it was the definitive work on the Texas Longhorn, and it remains so today. If you want to understand the Longhorn in depth, I heartily recommend Dobie's book. I also acknowledge my debt to Mr. Dobie for many of the ideas and insights expressed in the following pages.

J. Frank Dobie did more—much more—than just write about Longhorns, however. He was one of the principal figures involved in helping save the breed from extinction back in the 1930s. We will touch on that again later, but suffice it to say that I would not have had the life-changing privilege and experience of working with the Texas Longhorn had it not been for Dobie's untiring devotion to the cause.

At the Fort Griffin State Historic Park, where I also serve as park manager, we sell a number of excellent books about Texas and Western history, and I have a great appreciation for the written word. Take time to read a good book.

I would encourage you to start with *The Longhorns* by J. Frank Dobie.

Seek Advice

When I became manager of the State Herd in 1972, I wanted to learn everything I could about the Longhorns. I had worked around cattle all my life, but not Longhorns specifically.

I needed to know their distinctive characteristics, what made them different from other breeds. I wanted to make sure that the Longhorns in our herd were authentic Longhorns.

Garnett Brooks was president of the Cowboy Hall of Fame in Oklahoma City and had been an inspector for the Texas Longhorn Breeders Association of America. Garnett knew Longhorns, and I called to ask if I could go visit him.

He said he would come to Fort Griffin instead. He wanted to see the cattle first-hand, so he could point out their physical characteristics to me. He came three times and also brought some old photographs taken in the early 1900s. The information and advice he gave was invaluable.

I have always appreciated Garnett's willingness to go beyond the call of duty to help a young man who was just starting out. Early on in my association with Longhorns, I learned the value of seeking—and respecting—good advice.

Make a Good First Impression

It's something we try to instill in our children, especially when they are meeting someone for the first time, or going for a job or scholarship interview. Make a good first impression. Dress appropriately. Shake hands firmly. Make eye contact. Be polite. Exude confidence, but don't be cocky.

When it comes to first impressions, I don't know of any creature who does it more naturally than the Texas Longhorn. I have watched the expressions on the faces of literally thousands of people who are seeing Longhorns up close for the first time. Invariably, they are impressed. No, they are overwhelmed.

Once, I was accompanying a touring group of senior citizens at the park, and I radioed ahead for an assistant to bring the cattle up so they would be running across the road as we left the park. On the trip out to the park, the tourists were tired and didn't have much to say. But after seeing the Longhorns, they were enthusiastic and couldn't stop talking about them.

Don't underestimate the importance of making a good first impression. It can make friends and open doors.

5

MAKE A LASTING IMPRESSION

EVEN AFTER MORE THAN THIRTY YEARS of working with Longhorns, I am still awed by their majesty, their elegance, their beauty, their strength, and their individuality.

The new doesn't wear off. They never become commonplace. I don't take them for granted.

First impressions are important. Lasting impressions are testimony to true character.

BE A CHAMPION

IN 1987, TWO OF THE LONGHORN COWS from the State Herd won world championships. Lady Luck was named the World Grand Champion Longhorn Cow, and Lady Griffin was selected World Grand Champion Senior Longhorn Cow.

Longhorn competitions and shows are held throughout the United States and Canada. Hundreds of breeders compete for top prizes, and the best of the best gather for championship shows in Fort Worth, Texas, in June.

Competition—whether it involves Longhorns or people—is healthy when it makes us strive to do our best, to improve, to be stronger. Winning, however, should always be the byproduct of competition, not the overriding goal.

We all are champions when we do our best.

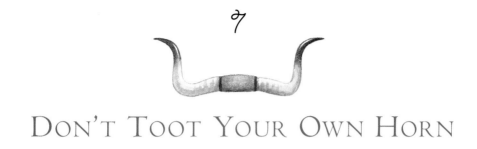

Don't Toot Your Own Horn

It is impossible for a Longhorn to toot his own horn.

We humans don't seem to have any trouble doing so.

BE COURAGEOUS

I CANNOT THINK OF A SINGLE TIME that I have ever seen a Longhorn intimidated by anything. When handled and cared for by man, they become gentle and tame animals, but if provoked, cornered, or threatened, they will stand their ground. They have even been known to fight wolves, panthers, even grizzlies—and win.

Of course, it helps if you weigh two thousand pounds and carry around on your head a five-foot-long lethal weapon. But a lot of it has to do with attitude. When they were wild, Longhorns had to be tough to survive, and that trait has been passed down through the years.

A sportswear company proclaims its slogan on TV commercials: "No fear."

Longhorns have no fear.

There may be a time in your life when you are called on to exhibit Longhorn courage.

For some young people, it comes when they risk their lives to defend their country, their freedom, their way of life. For others, it comes when they rush into a burning building to rescue a child. Or maybe it is the quiet courage of doing a job well every day because that is what is expected. Or standing up for someone who can't stand up for himself. Or taking an unpopular position because you feel it is the right thing to do. Or maybe *not* taking a position, but rather letting someone else have the final say.

Longhorn courage takes a variety of shapes.

9

BE CAPTAIN OF YOUR SOUL

IF IT HADN'T BEEN FOR THE TEXAS LONGHORNS, the great cattle drives of the 1870s and 1880s would not have been possible. Only the tough Longhorns were capable of enduring the grueling thousand-mile treks to market.

J. Frank Dobie called them "the cattle of the hour." He said, "They suited the wide, untamed land and the men that ranged it."

I like his description of the physical and spiritual attributes of the Longhorn. No one ever said it better or more succinctly than Dobie did in this passage from *The Longhorns:*

> "With their steel hoofs, their long legs, their staglike muscles, their thick skins, their powerful horns, they could walk the roughest ground, cross the widest deserts, climb the highest mountains, swim the widest rivers, fight off the fiercest band of wolves, endure hunger, cold, thirst, and punishment as few beasts of the earth have ever shown themselves capable of enduring. On the prairies they could run like antelopes; in the thickets of thorn and tangle they could break their way with the agility of panthers. They could rustle in drouth or snow, smell out pasturage leagues away, live—without talking about the matter—like true captains of their own souls and bodies."

10

MAKE HISTORY COME ALIVE

WHEN I SAY THE TEXAS LONGHORN is a *living legacy,* what I mean is the Longhorn is a direct, living, in-the-flesh connection to our past.

The Longhorn makes the history of the West come alive. You can read about the trail drives and the beginning of the cattle industry, but when you have seen live Longhorns, the words jump off the page. They become real flesh and blood and horn.

I enjoy historical reenactments and find they are a way to make our history meaningful. But every day, I am reminded that history is right in front of me in the State Longhorn Herd.

"The Texas Longhorn," said Dobie, "made more history than any other breed of cattle the civilized world has known."

I encourage you not only to study history, but also to experience it. Share it with your children. Pass along the colorful heritage of the American West, a heritage that is embodied in the living legend, the Texas Longhorn.

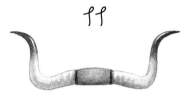

BE SELF-SUFFICIENT

LONGHORNS ARE FULLY CAPABLE of taking care of themselves.

Now that may seem odd coming from a guy who makes his living tending to Longhorns. But throughout history—and even today—the Longhorn has been a hearty, self-sufficient animal.

Longhorns can make it on their own better than any other breed of cattle I know. At the state parks where the State Herd makes its home, we provide some feed and see that adequate water is available. I can call the cattle, and they will come running if they think I am going to feed them. They have been trained to do so.

But left on their own, Longhorns will fend for themselves. I remember one time during a bitter ice storm that lasted for days everything was covered with a layer of ice. The cattle couldn't graze, and we couldn't get a truck into the pasture to take feed to them.

The Longhorns survived by browsing on scrubs and trees.

These days most of us have it pretty easy in our lives. We don't have to be nearly as self-sufficient or as resourceful as our ancestors were. In many ways, we've become soft. But when we have to confront a major change in the landscape of our lives, as we all do from time to time, we will be better able to cope if we nourish—in ourselves and in our children—the value of self-sufficiency, the ability to take care of ourselves.

DON'T TAKE WATER FOR GRANTED

LONGHORNS DRINK A LOT OF WATER—when it is available. In observing them, I estimate the average Longhorn drinks twenty-five gallons of water a day.

And yet, they can go without water for several days if they have to, and they are more capable of surviving drought than other cattle because they are more wide-ranging. They will seek out water no matter how far they have to travel to get to it.

Like the Longhorn, those of us who live in the more arid sections of the country have had to learn how to endure periods of drought. With a little rain, the ecosystem of the Plains thrives—producing bountiful grass, productive land, and healthy livestock. But when rain is lacking, one has to be tough and resourceful to survive.

We watch the skies, the natural signs, and the weather forecasts hopefully, even prayerfully. And we never take water for granted.

13

BE TRUE TO YOUR SCHOOL

THE LONGHORN IS THE MASCOT FOR MORE than twenty high schools in Texas, and another half-dozen schools call themselves Steers. There are Longhorns at high schools in California, Colorado, Wyoming, Montana, Nebraska, Kansas, Tennessee, and Ohio. A Canadian rugby team calls itself the Longhorns.

The most famous Longhorns are the ones at the University of Texas, personified by a real, live Texas Longhorn named Bevo. Several of the Bevo mascots have come from the State Herd.

"Hook 'em Horns" is the spirit cry at the University of Texas. The hand gesture, made by extending the forefinger and little finger and folding the other two fingers under the thumb, closely resembles the skull of a Longhorn. UT student Henry Pitts—who now lives in College Station, by the way—discovered it in 1955, while making hand shadow figures on the wall in his dorm. He shared his discovery with cheerleader Harley Clark, who introduced the salute at a pep rally. It caught on immediately.

When you talk about Texas Longhorns, it's not always clear whether you mean the sports team or the cattle breed, just as it is sometimes confusing whether a reference to the Texas Rangers these days means law enforcement or baseball.

I was once asked to speak to a group about the Texas Longhorns. I launched into a little history of the Longhorns and started telling about some of the distinctive characteristics of the breed. I noticed that I was losing my audience. They looked confused. I stopped and asked what was wrong.

A man spoke up, "We thought you were here to talk about the Texas Longhorns football team."

14

VALUE YOUR GOOD NAME

WE SHOULD LIVE OUR LIVES so that our name would be worthy of emulation.

Certainly that is true of the Longhorn name. It is a good name, a proud name—a name that evokes strength, tradition, pride, and trust.

It shouldn't come as a surprise that hundreds, if not thousands, of businesses have chosen to use the word Longhorn in their business name. A check of just three cities—Houston, Austin, and Fort Worth—found these examples, to name only a few:

Longhorn Auto Sales. Longhorn Bail Bonds. Longhorn Boat and Camper. Longhorn Café. Longhorn Cleaners. Longhorn Dental. Longhorn Dodge. Longhorn Electric. Longhorn Feed & Seed. Longhorn Fence. Longhorn Glass. Longhorn Limousines. Long Horn Meat Market. Longhorn Mortgage. Longhorn Moving. Longhorn Nail Salon. Longhorn Painting. Longhorn Pet Supply. Longhorn Publishing. Longhorn Roofing. Longhorn Saloon. Longhorn Steel. Longhorn Storage. Longhorn Termite & Pest Control. Longhorn Tire Center. Longhorn Trophies.

And one more: The Longhorn Council, Boy Scouts of America, serves youth in twenty-three counties in North and Central Texas.

15

APPRECIATE A SUNRISE

I ENJOY DRIVING THROUGH FORT GRIFFIN STATE PARK early in the morning and watching the sunrise. The glistening of the rays reflected off the raised horns of the cattle is a spectacular sight to behold.

You don't have to be at a state park or with a herd of Longhorns to appreciate a good sunrise. Just get up in the quiet of the morning and observe the wonders of nature unfold before your eyes, then remind yourself that of all the sunrises you will see in your lifetime there will never be another exactly like that one.

SAVOR A SUNSET

I TAKE A LOT OF PHOTOGRAPHS OF SUNSETS. Some of my favorite pictures have been Longhorns on a slight rise in the landscape, silhouetted against the setting sun.

With few trees or mountains to get in the way, West Texas sunsets take their time reaching a grand finale. They suggest to us that too often we rush through our lives in such a hurry that we miss the beauty, the grandeur, the romance, the art of living.

Great moments, like great sunsets, should be savored.

SING TO SOOTHE THE SOUL

DURING THE GREAT CATTLE DRIVES, cowboys riding guard at night would try to keep the Longhorns calm and peaceful by singing to them. The cattle could easily be spooked into a stampede by sudden noises, and the voices of singing cowboys had a soothing effect.

They sang songs like "Get Along Little Dogie," "Dan Tucker," "When the Work's All Done This Fall," "Bury Me Not on the Lone Prairie," "Red River Valley," "Streets of Laredo," "Goodbye Old Paint," "Little Joe the Wrangler," and "The Texas Lullaby." They sang hymns like "Nearer My God to Thee," "In the Sweet By and By," and "Rock of Ages."

Longhorns still enjoy cowboy songs. It doesn't really matter how well the cowboy can sing, or whether he knows a lot of songs by heart, or just dozens of verses of the same song. A ballad, a lullaby, a hymn soothes the soul.

It works well with children, too.

RECITE A FAVORITE VERSE

WHEN IT COMES TO SINGING THE PRAISES of the Texas Longhorn as the State Animal of Texas, I am rather partial to the poem, "Cattle," by Berta Hart Nance, which begins so appropriately this way:

Other states were carved or born;

Texas grew from hide and horn.

Other states are long and wide;

Texas is a shaggy hide.

And a little farther down, there is this verse:

Other soil is full of stones;

Texans plow up cattle bones.

The poem, I believe, captures in a few words the essence of the Longhorn's influence in the development of the state's history, culture, and economy.

MAKE BABIES

LONGHORNS HAVE AN EASIER TIME GIVING BIRTH than most breeds because their calves are smaller in proportion and easier to drop. Longhorn bulls are popular choices for breeding first-calf heifers of other breeds because the small size of the calf better ensures a successful delivery.

Longhorn cows practice natural childbirth. In my thirty-plus years with the State Herd, I don't recall ever having to pull a Longhorn calf. One cow in our herd had a calf every year for twenty-eight consecutive years. (Unlike the Longhorns, we humans don't need to be anywhere near that prolific.)

A visitor asked me one time, "When do they get their horns?"

"They are born with them," I replied. The calves have little nubs, or buttons, at birth, but apparently I didn't make that clear.

"My," the woman exclaimed, "I bet that is rough on the cow." She envisioned the calves being born with full-grown horns.

Now that would be painful!

TAKE CARE OF YOUR CHILDREN

LONGHORN COWS ARE GREAT MOTHERS.

They staunchly defend and protect their calves. They can outrun and outfight wolves, coyotes, and other predators. They are great babysitters, coddlers, and nurturers. In cold weather, I've seen them round up their calves and stay with them. If you are trying to separate a cow from her calf, you had better be prepared to climb a tree if she catches you.

A Longhorn cow will use deception to hide a calf. With other breeds, you can follow a cow and she will lead you to her calf. Not so with Longhorns. A Longhorn cow might go in the opposite direction of where the calf is to throw you off the trail, then double back when you get tired of following.

If you thought your mother was fiercely protective, perhaps she had learned something from Longhorns.

REMEMBER THE WAY HOME

LONGHORNS ARE CREATURES OF HABIT. They will range far afield to find food and water, but they like to return to familiar surroundings.

Like a baseball player, they instinctively head for home.

The most famous story concerns Sancho, who was raised as a pet Longhorn steer south of San Antonio. In 1880, Sancho was rounded up with other Longhorns and driven to Wyoming. All along the way, Sancho would lag behind and look back. Several times he tried to walk off.

Finally, after several months, the cattle arrived in Wyoming, where they were rebranded with the new owner's brand.

The cowboys returned home. The next spring they were shocked to see Sancho—bearing both his Texas and Wyoming brands—back at the South Texas cabin where he had grown up. He never left home again.

22

MAKE A COMEBACK

IF YOU'VE EVER FAILED AT SOMETHING—and who among us hasn't—it doesn't have to be the last word. You have the potential to make a comeback.

Longhorns did. The breed, which had dominated the open range in the 1860s and 1870s, was on the verge of extinction by 1920. The closing of the open range, several brutal winters, changes in breed preferences among cowmen, and other factors had led to the Longhorns' decline.

In 1927, Senator John B. Kendrick of Wyoming convinced Congress to appropriate $3,000 to preserve the Longhorn by establishing a federal herd at the Wichita Mountains Wildlife Refuge in Oklahoma. Will Barnes and John H. Hatton found twenty cows, three bulls, and four calves.

The comeback had begun. In 1964, the Texas Longhorn Breeders Association of America was founded by a few ranchers who joined together to preserve the breed and promote its qualities. At the time, there were just a few hundred Longhorns worthy of the name. Today the TLBAA has 5,000 members, and there are more than 300,000 registered Longhorns.

For more details on the association, based in Fort Worth, visit its web site at www.tlbaa.org.

23

DEVOTE YOURSELF TO A CAUSE

IN THE 1930s, FORT WORTH BUSINESSMAN SID RICHARDSON became convinced that the Longhorn was closer to extinction than the buffalo. He put up the money to assemble a State Longhorn Herd.

J. Frank Dobie enlisted the help of longtime cattle detective, rancher, and Longhorn specialist, Graves Peeler, to round up the initial herd. Peeler dedicated himself to the task, traveling all over the state and into Mexico to find cattle with the appropriate characteristics.

Peeler's story is related in an excellent little book by Lawrence Clayton, *Longhorn Legacy: Graves Peeler and the Texas Cattle Trade.*

"The task was not easy," Clayton wrote. "Before he died, Peeler amassed the largest herd of Longhorn cattle in the world. The registry of this most Western of all breeds of cattle would not have been possible without the efforts of this rare individual."

Many of the Longhorns in the State of Texas Herd today trace their lineage to the original cattle purchased by Peeler. The Longhorn became his legacy, and thanks to him it has become my life's work as well.

Graves Peeler was the right man at the right time for the right cause. He seized the opportunity and made a difference.

Promote Tourism

THE CATTLE IN THE STATE LONGHORN HERD at Fort Griffin are great ambassadors for Fort Griffin, for Texas, and for America. They draw visitors from all over the world.

That hasn't always been the case. When the herd was first established, the Longhorns weren't so popular. The first State Herd was taken to Lake Corpus Christi State Park. As additional cattle were rounded up, they were placed at Lake Brownwood State Park. But park patrons at both locations were uneasy about the cattle being there. At Corpus, a steer once helped himself to a baked ham off a picnic table. At Brownwood, neighboring ranchers worried that the Longhorns would escape and mix with their cattle.

The Brownwood cattle were sent to Lake Corpus Christi and, in 1948, the Longhorns at Corpus were rounded up. Twenty-one were shipped to Fort Griffin State Park, the remainder sold. Since then, the herd has prospered and grown, both in the number of Longhorns and in their popularity.

Today, they are featured attractions not only at Fort Griffin, but also at San Angelo, Abilene, Copper Breaks, Palo Duro Canyon, Lake Colorado City, and Possum Kingdom State Parks.

FIND YOUR NICHE

TEXAS LONGHORNS HAVE FOUND THEIR NICHE in the cattle industry because of their strengths as breeding and beef animals. Some of the distinguishing characteristics of the breed are:

- Ease of calving
- Production of lean beef
- Forage well on poor range
- Adapt to various climates
- Resistance to disease
- Require low maintenance

Longhorns aren't for everyone and may not be the best breed for every occasion or need. But they have a niche, they have an important role, and they make an important contribution.

So do we. Our niche may be as visionary, organizer, or worker; as leader or team player; as friend, supporter, or encourager; as server, problem-solver, or caregiver. Whatever you do well, that's where you can find your niche.

26

SCRATCH WHAT ITCHES

ONE OF THE ADVANTAGES OF HAVING long horns is that it makes it easy for a Longhorn to scratch.

We all have itches to scratch—and not just physically. We may have the itch to get into a more satisfying line of work. We may have the itch to go back to school. We may have the itch to become part of a greater cause, to do something worthwhile in our community. We may have the itch to find more spiritual depth, more meaning, more purpose, more beauty in our lives.

Find the itch that needs scratching and, like the Longhorn, don't just let it itch. Take action. Scratch.

27

DON'T MEASURE YOUR WORTH IN MONEY

IN THE EARLY DAYS OF THE REPUBLIC OF TEXAS, a hundred-dollar bank note pictured a Longhorn steer being chased by a horse and rider.

Back then, cattle were actually worth more than the money they were printed on. The money was virtually worthless, but a cow and calf were valuable commodities.

After all, you couldn't eat the money.

Still can't.

28

Eat Lean Beef

When he was a hundred years old, Isom Like—an old Indian-fighter and horse trader—was asked his secret for living so long.

"Live temperately in food and drinks," he said. "Try to get your beefsteaks three times a day, fried in taller [tallow]. Taller is mighty healing, and there's nothing like it to keep your stumich [sic] greased-up and in good working order."

I'm rather certain that modern medicine would frown on that diet. One advantage of Longhorn beef, which has made the breed more popular for health-conscious Americans, is that it is leaner and lower in cholesterol than most beef.

Lean Longhorn beef, says Dr. Joseph Graham, a cardiovascular surgeon and a Longhorn breeder, is on a par with skinned, boneless white chicken meat.

Longhorn beef is not widely available. The Texas Longhorn Breeders Association of America says it can be found in select supermarkets and restaurants or from breeders who market their own beef.

GET PLENTY OF EXERCISE

IN THE OLD DAYS, YOU DIDN'T SEE many fat Longhorns. They were too busy walking, climbing, running, fighting. They got an abundance of exercise.

Even today, under much more controlled and favorable conditions, they cover more range than other cattle. Longhorns are leaner than most breeds—hence, the leaner meat with less cholesterol. They may be pampered by comparison with their ancestors, but they still get plenty of exercise.

30

PREVENT STAMPEDES

A MAJOR CONCERN ON THE CATTLE DRIVES was the stampede, and Longhorns were more inclined to stampede than other breeds. They were naturally wary animals, extremely sensitive to thunder and lightning, sudden noises or movements, stray dogs, even a cowboy's sneeze.

"The best way to manage a stampede," wrote J. Frank Dobie, "was to prevent it. A good herd boss would not bed his cattle on ground that sounded hollow, in a narrow valley, or on a rough point. He picked, if possible, the kind of level ground the cattle would pick for themselves for a bed… He watered the cattle thoroughly and saw that they got their fill of grass before lying down.

In other words, the boss treated the cattle with respect, treated them as he would want to be treated. Good advice for bosses, even today, for preventing stampedes at work.

31

DON'T MICRO-MANAGE

SOME BOSSES HAVE AN ANNOYING TENDENCY to micro-manage—that is, they need to control everything that goes on, make every decision, approve every purchase.

With the State Herd, we try to manage the Longhorns, but it's virtually impossible to micro-manage. They are independent creatures.

Once, a movie crew was out at the state park shooting footage of the Longhorns for a scene in their movie. At one point, the director wasn't satisfied with exactly where the Longhorns had stationed themselves. He asked me, "Could you move this one over that way just a little—and that one over this way a few feet—and that one a few feet that way?"

Well, no, I couldn't. And didn't.

EMBRACE VARIETY AND INDIVIDUALITY

THE LONGHORN IS THE ONLY BREED that has the variety or range in colors that you find in people. Another reason why it is the All-American breed. No two Longhorns look exactly alike. They have different shapes and sizes of horns. They have, I know, different personalities—or should I say Longhornalities?

And so it is with us. We are individuals, each of us unique in our own way, with our own unique qualities, interests, and abilities. We don't all look alike or act alike. Thank goodness.

Have Something to Say

LONGHORNS TALK. I know they do, because I hear them all the time.

Maybe not in words exactly. But through a variety of vocal tones, Longhorns can get their point across very clearly. I don't know of another breed with such a variety of expressions.

Longhorns have different tones for calling a baby calf or an older calf, for when they are distressed or angry, for when they are thirsty or satisfied.

When Longhorns speak, they have something to say. It's a good lesson for the rest of us.

34

LEAVE SOMETHING BEHIND

EVEN AFTER A LONGHORN HAS DIED, part of him stays behind. A steer may become someone's dinner. The hide has a variety of uses. But the most lasting legacy is the Longhorn's horns.

Displayed on a wall or as a centerpiece of Western or Southwestern décor, the horns continue to be impressive, long after the Longhorn is but a memory. They help create an aura that links the past to the present and preserves the lore, the heritage, and the romance of the Old West.

It is testimony to the dignity, the grace, and the majesty of the Longhorn that even after death, his legacy lives on.

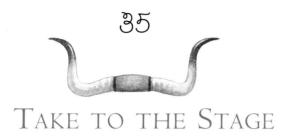

35

TAKE TO THE STAGE

LONGHORNS ARE STARS OF STAGE AND SCREEN. For years they have played major supporting roles in a variety of Western movies—not all of them historically accurate.

In Albany, Texas, they have a featured part every summer in the outdoor musical, *The Fort Griffin Fandangle.* They have been performing live at *Fandangle* for more than fifty years.

On cue, fifteen to twenty Longhorns from the State Herd make their exciting entrance, running down the hill onto the outdoor stage, driven by cowboys. They make the most of their time in the spotlight by just being themselves while a cowboy on horseback sings a lullaby to them. As the song is ending, the Longhorns, who know their part well, pause for a moment as if to relish the applause, then dash offstage and back to their quarters.

Even if you've seen the musical every year for thirty or forty years, you can't help but be impressed by the way the Longhorns steal the show.

DON'T BE DIFFICULT

Even though they once were wild, Longhorns these days are more likely to be rather gentle—unless threatened.

I have found Longhorns to be intelligent, easy to handle, easy to work.

In the old days, their wildness was important to their survival. They had to fend for themselves.

These days, their docility is one of the reasons the breed has made a successful comeback. Longhorns have learned how to get along.

37

LEARN TO SWIM

LONGHORNS ARE EXCELLENT SWIMMERS. During the trail drives, they would plunge into raging, icy rivers and come out fine on the other side.

The most incredible story I heard about Longhorns swimming was told by a cowboy who worked on a large ranch in Texas.

The ranch bought a small herd of Longhorns and put them in a fenced pasture. A few days later, the cattle had crossed the fence and were in the adjoining pasture. They couldn't find any gates open or any gaps in the fence. So they moved the Longhorns back to their original pasture. A few days later they were back across the fence.

This went on for several months. The cowboys decided someone must be moving the cattle as a prank.

Finally, they decided to watch and see if they could determine how the cattle were getting across the fence. They were astonished to see the Longhorns go into a tank for a drink, dive under the water, swim under the fence, and come up on the other side.

Frankly, I thought the cowboy was pulling my leg. So I called the ranch foreman, and he said that's exactly what happened.

Swimming is a survival skill we all should master. It might be the difference between life and death.

38

ADAPT TO YOUR SURROUNDINGS

I HAVE BEEN FORTUNATE TO BE in the same job, at the same place, for more than thirty years. I haven't wanted to move around, and I haven't had to.

That used to be the way most people lived. They were born, grew up, lived, and died in roughly the same place, usually not far from grandparents, aunts, uncles, and cousins.

These days, that kind of stability is more the exception than the rule. We've become a mobile society, and, as such, we find ourselves having to adapt to new people, new customs, new ideas, new cultures. Even if we stay in the same place, we are likely to encounter new bosses and new ways of doing things.

Change can be stressful or it can be exhilarating, or both. One of the strengths of the Longhorn over the years has been his ability to adapt to different climates, different terrains, different situations. The Longhorn found a way to adapt and survive without changing the essential character of who he is.

39

BE CURIOUS

LONGHORNS ARE INQUISITIVE. They seem to be as interested in observing us as we are in observing them.

I was showing a visitor around the state park. He followed me in his car as I drove my pickup out to a pasture and called the Longhorns in so he could have a closer look. He got out, and as he took photographs, a couple of calves walked up to his car, sniffed at the door handle, and licked it to see how it tasted.

Once, I was out in the field shooting pictures when I caught a glimpse of a Longhorn calf sniffing the red fruit of a prickly pear. I snapped off a shot without even aiming, and it later won a photo contest.

Take it from the Longhorn. Develop an inquisitive mind. Be interested in what is going on around you.

NEVER STOP GROWING

A LONGHORN'S HORNS NEVER STOP growing until the animal dies.
Never stop growing: Good advice for us as well.

Be Supportive

We have a fairly new program, called the Adopt-A-Longhorn Project, in which we invite people to make donations to help with the care and feeding of the State Longhorn Herd, located at Fort Griffin State Park.

In return for a donation of $25 to $500 and up, the donor gets to name a Longhorn calf. We ask donors to submit a first choice and a second choice for the name.

Once the name has been approved, we send you a picture of your Longhorn, a copy of the registration papers featuring the Longhorn's approved name, and a certificate recognizing your contribution to the Adopt-A-Longhorn Project.

It's a way to help ensure that the Longhorn herd will continue to thrive, and it's a pretty neat gift idea. For more information, come by the park or contact us by phone at (325) 762-3592 or by mail at 1701 North U.S. Highway 283, Albany, Texas 76430.

Living with Longhorns

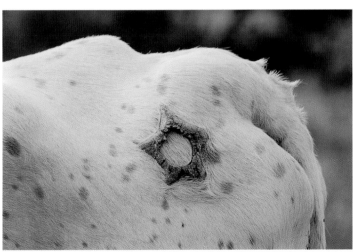